"Zen is to have the
heart and soul of a little child."

—TAKAUN

ZEN and the Art of Changing Diapers

Sarah Arsone

LOS ANGELES / 1993

First, 1991
Second edition, revised, 1993

Published by Sarah Arsone
P.O. Box 1486
Pacific Palisades, California 90272

ISBN 0-9632721-0-1
Library of Congress No. 92-093905

Design and typography by Jim Cook
Printed and bound in the United States of America

For Carol, Rachel, and Evan

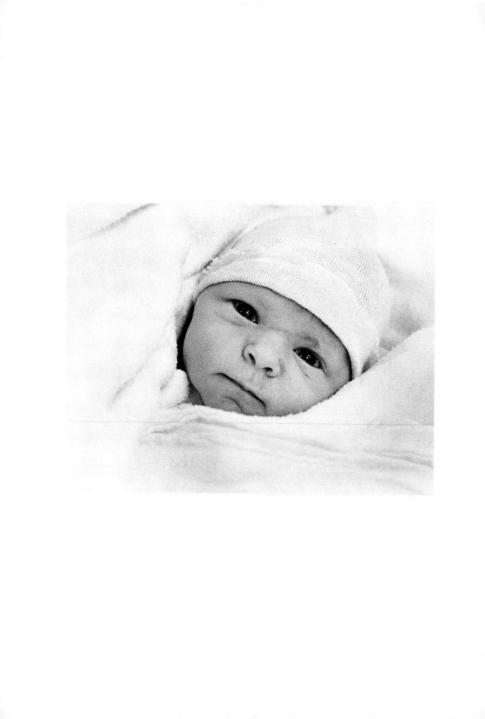

"And no grownup will ever understand
that this is a matter of such importance."

ANTOINE DE SAINT-EXUPÉRY

Table of Contents

Photographs:

BY LISE ALEXANDER:
   And No Grownup Will Ever Understand
   A Father's Poem
   A Wild Patience

COVER PHOTOGRAPH BY THE AUTHOR, Just Listen.

Acknowledgements

I would like to thank all the friends and colleagues who so generously shared their stories with me and contributed as well the talent, knowledge, support, praise, criticism, and encouragement that made the writing, publishing, and marketing of this book possible: Lise Alexander, Michael Andrews and Jack Grapes at Bombshelter Press, Randall Beek at Bookpeople. Bob Brown, Judith Dykstra Brown, Elizabeth Busick, Rita Catanzerite. The Group: Idelle Davidson, Kathy Seal, Cherri Senders, Charlene Marmar Solomon, Julie Wheelock, Kathryn Phillips. Jane English at Earth Heart Press. Catherine Fernandes, Frances Fernandes, Beverly Feinstein. Magda Gerber, Carol Pinto and Patty Feder at Resources for Infant Educarers, (R.I.E.) as well as all the staff, parents and kids at R.I.E. Judith Hawkins at New Leaf. Robin Johnson, Kei Kanishiro, David Lawrence, Barbara Lombardo, Diana Mathers, Amy McCurdy, Evan and Rachel Pinto, Judy Saxon. Joyce B. Schwartz, and Robin Liberman Schyman at the *Sculpture Gardens Review* and Sculpture Gardens poetry reading series. Alan Steed, Mary Streit, Paula Thompson, Carol Spivik Weinstock, Jon Winokur.

"The only certainty is change,
and the art of changing is all
we can really cling to."

LA-SOEN

Preface

A couple of years ago a leading women's magazine hired me to write an article about diapering. My resulting journalistic presentation was typically crisp, brief, and pointed. However, it seemed to lack something. I wanted to do more. I wanted to put soul into the subject. I wanted the reader to really feel it.

As I meditated on the material, I decided to write a love poem from a father to his new-born daughter. Poetry, I reasoned, offers an opportunity for the reader to experience a subject rather than just read about it.

In my poem, I apply Zen ideas as a set of philosophical brakes slowing down a fast-paced dad caring for his baby. Zen masters say that instead of charging ahead, a Zen student "just" sits and breathes. (The "just" is an inside Zen joke because, although "just" sitting sounds simple, it turns out to be hard enough to warrant a lifetime of meditation practice.) By sitting still and observing the breath, the Zen practitioner is said to experience the true natural order of the universe. She or he can then understand and work within the framework of that order instead of trying to fight it. "You just sit. But the calmness of your sitting will encourage you in your everyday life," wrote Shunryu Suzuki.

In the most simple way, sitting can lead to great things. With Zen, grandeur exists in everything: An exquisite sunrise or a simple human chore. A diamond or a clod of dirt. Zen finds the miraculous in the ordinary. The Zen poet P'ang-yun wrote: "How wondrously supernatural! And how miraculous this is! I draw water, and I carry wood!"

Of course, the pattern of ordinary daily American life does not usually include carrying around buckets of water and cords of fire wood. And "just" sitting to the busy parents of young children really is a joke. However, we do have babies to keep us in touch with the most humble and ordinary tasks and natural rhythms.

The demands of children also have a special way of waking us up to life. They open our eyes. At times, children may belt out a loud wake-up call in the middle of the night. Other times, they may open our eyes to the delight of seeing things from the infant's point of view for the very first time. "Zen is simply a voice crying, 'Wake up! Wake up!'" wrote Maha Sthavira Sangharakshita.

A Zen master asks those who would wake up to Satori, or sudden enlightenment, to solve a koan. (We have all heard the famous koan, "What is the sound of one hand clapping?") A koan is a problem to which there is no logical solution. Such unsolvable puzzles are meant to collapse the usual rigid structure of thought and let Satori rush in. A baby, too, is a kind of koan, designed by nature to pull the rug out from under parents' feet, to bring them enlightenment as well as love if they are willing to "just" listen.

SARAH ARSONE

A Father's Poem

All life
is change
and nobody
knows it
better than you,
Babe, with your
mutable moods
and endless diapers,
teaching me
to let go
of desires
fixed by clocks
and deals
and move in time
to your smiles
and squalls,
your needs for food
and drink
while
my strong arms hold
your delicate shape
against my heart.

While changing you,
I love the special moments
we have together
when our bodies
are close
and I look into
your eyes.

I remember when you
were six weeks old
and as I was changing you
you smiled at me
for the first time
saying with your grin
Thanks, Dad, for
taking care of me.

That sweet curve
of your lips
melted me down
to the same
soft bones I had
when I was a baby.

With you, I'm starting
to see the whole world
over again as fresh as
the first time I saw it.
You're waking me up.

At night, you simply rouse me
with the sound of your cries
as I stumble in my sleepy way
to see what you need.

You also make
me wake
to all of life
with the moves
you take
creeping, crawling
seeing and touching
mouthing everything
feeling and tasting
what this original world
offers you.

I love looking at
the beautiful smile
on your face and all
those expressions
which move through you
like water flowing down
a river course
in bubbling gladness
or stormy squall.

One minute you lie
sleeping quiet as an
autumn pool, the next
awake and wild
as white-water rapids
while I struggle
to understand
what's bothering you.

I ask "What is it, Babe?"
But you just cry and cry
and make your baffling,
baby sounds.

Could it be
hunger or gas,
an open diaper pin
sticking in
your tender new skin,
or some noise
that scared you?
I investigate
every clue
like Sherlock Holmes
and Watson too.

I sniff your diapers
then, my mind races
back to the scene
of your breakfast
to calculate
if it could be
what you ate.

I practice
every way I know
holding, rocking, singing
feeding, changing
to comfort you.

Before you came
I thought
changing diapers
would be just
boring drudgery
like any
tiresome chore
like mopping a floor
over and over
again.

But with you
the most
ordinary things
refresh me
in a way
I never knew
before,
and think
I could
never learn
without you.

At changing time
when I'm here
with you near
sometimes I see everything
so clear, I swear
I even see the air
you move with your waving
hands and feet
while I make sure
your diaper is soft
and the water
I bathe you in is not
too cold or too hot,
because no small detail
touching you is boring
or unimportant.

Suddenly everything matters
however humble.
Even your unlovely
daily poop and drool
and spit up all count
for something.

While waiting
for you to be born
my imagination
soared high as stars
light years away
from the most simple Zen
of loving you.

I flew far off in thought
to dream of your
future glories.
I was already
choosing between
Stanford, Harvard
and Yale for you.

In my mind's eye
I dressed up
in black tie and tux
to take Mommy in her long,
gold glittering, shimmering gown
to your inaugural ball
on the White House lawn.

But changing
smelly diapers
Disgusting!
Not for me.
No part of
wondrous fantasy
I thought,
before you came.

Just plain stink
it seemed,
a common price to pay
for having you—
like mother's pain
or the grim hospital stay.

Well, you're here now
and you're mine.
To my delight
nothing about you
is disgusting—
not even your diapers.

And the risks
you take,
thrill
and
frighten me
as much as
Evel Knievel
flying
on his
motorcycle
through
hoops
of flame.

Like
the day
you crawled down
the front porch
stairs
and I was afraid
you'd fall
and break your neck.

But you were
all confidence
and poise,
perfectly balanced
like you were
trying out
for a job
as a Hollywood
stunt baby.

I saw a look of
complete
concentration
on your face
like a two-foot-long
Einstein
working on
some problem
huge as you
are small
and I trusted you
and let you go.

You're beautiful.

But you're
not just
a pretty picture babe
like that precious
tiny girl
we once saw
dressed
in Victorian
lace
lying so still
in her antique
cradle
I thought
she was
a china doll.

You are
no little
stiff princess
still life.

You are beauty
in motion
—exploring everywhere.

You raise
your head up to see
how the fly flies in the air.

When he walks on the lawn
you stoop to catch him there.
But he's already gone.

So you stay
down
touching the place
where he was
with your hand
feeling around
to learn
the language of grass
blade by blade.

You're teaching me
to slow down.
With you, I forget
to rush after things
that used to seem
so important—like
training for
the Marathon,
or more and better
business deals—
new automobiles.

When I see your eyes
simply following
the flight of the moth
from ceiling to wall
I promise not to hurry you
away from sights like this.
I take the time
to watch too
together with you.

You inspect
your toes
and through
your eyes,
toes look new
to me too,
as if I'd never seen
such a wonderful
invention before.

And the small
particles you touch:

the cat's fur
or carpet nap,
motes of dust
floating down
a sunbeam's path
into your hand
all seem wondrous new
as I discover them
with you.

Your mouth is
still too young
to manufacture
English words,
but excellent
at making
drool.

So long before
you converse
with us
humans
you and Shaggy Dog
love a good bark
together.

And your way
with the dog
makes me
lose
my cool
reserve.

You get so good
at doggie talk
you give an
ARF ARF ARF
with your
little voice
grown suddenly
so strong
and confident
it seems
you are
more Shaggy's pup
than my own child.

As you bark your way
through an evening romp,
I can't stop myself
from barking too
'til soon we were all—
baby, Shag and Dad,
playing wild
doggy games.

And I thought then
of the Zen
master SOEN
who wrote
so long ago
the poem of the
child and the dog
"Truly exorbitant,
their foolishness,
Being and non-being
annihilated!"

I know
now with you
what it is
to lose yourself
completely
to become one
with a dog
and his whirl
of animal
energy.

At bedtime
you were still
a clamoring puppy
who ran away when
I asked you to come
to me for a
diaper change—
wiggling,
squirming
to go free
and screaming
"NO! NO! NO"

I admit I yelled,
"Stay still,
Damnit
and do
it quick.
It's late
and time
for you
to sleep."

Then I stopped
to take in
some long,
deep breaths
of air,
and let them
out again
before
calmly asking you
to help me with
what must be done
—and you agreed.

I understood
how all
that wild river
of protest and fight
bursting out of you
made me reach deep
inside myself to find
peace enough
for both of us.

And that night
when I finally
got you changed
and down to sleep
I asked myself
why
such fierce
whirlwinds
swirl
inside of you,
my little babe,
who just twenty
months ago came
to light my life
with your gentle smile,
and wrapped
'round my big thumb
your tiny fingers—
trusting as
new spring vines
circling
a good old tree?

Or at least
I thought
you were asleep
as I laid beside
your dreaming mom
feeling my body
tired as old stones
in a dusty August river bed
with my mind wide awake
asking itself
again the question
why
those twisting winds
turn in you.

My brain
working overtime
searching for answers,
When I heard you
scream
from your crib
for "WATER!"

Oh,
I've had
enough
of you
for now.

I just
want you
to leave
me be
here
in my bed.

I want you to
stop
breaking
the night
silence
again
and again
with
your piercing
scream.

I turn over—
pull the blankets
'round my ears
to shut out
your sound
which rises
high
demanding my
attention
like megadecibil
rock 'n roll
and
brokenhearted
blues
or some
run-over
animal
wailing
a painful
dying song
I finally
can't ignore.

At last, you win.

I surrender
my need
for sleep
to your
nighttime cry
and
slip out
of bed
making
no sound or
extra moves
to
wake
your mom.

I go
into your
moonlit room
to find you standing
tear-streaked
in your crib.

I ask
what's
wrong?

You
say "WATER"
in a voice
too
strong.

But when
I hand you
the bottle
you pick it up
take half
a swallow
and send
it bouncing
to the floor
accompanied by
another roar
of "NO!"

Then, finding a store
of patience I
never knew before,
I ask your stuffed bear
to help us out.

I tell you
your soft Beary
says he's tired too
and wants to
go to sleep with you.

"NO!" you yell
wanting no part
of anything I offer you
not water, bear
or my soothing hug
that you wiggle out of
with a shrug
and again a
"NO!"

But you reach for
Beary anyway
wanting
his softness
that you see
even if the toy
comes from me.

You hold
Beary tight
then think
a moment
and take command
of all the animals
in your land,
ordering Bunny
and Tiger too—
All must now
come to bed
with you.

I bring them
like your
good lieutenant.

And you
demand I
put all
in a row
of perfect order:

First Bunny
then Beary
with Yellow Tiger last
—your troop
of pastel
soldiers
guarding you,
their captain,
on the first
night of your revolt.

At last,
you're quiet
and content
with cuddly beasts
to escort you
on your way
to a land of
baby sleep
where you dream
you're free
to get in
and out
of your crib
anytime
night or day
without a dad
or mom
or anyone else
to tell you
yes or nay.

Asleep, you climb the homey
mountains of your dreams.

First you mount
the changing table,
then conquer snowy peaks
of diaper stacks.

You ascend your toy chest
and stand there proud
on your own Everest
beneath the open window.

You stretch your arms
into the night
above your
safe and quiet room
to reach out to
the midnight sky
so bright and full of stars.

In my room
at last
I'm finally free
to sleep my sleep
and dream my own dreams
beside your mom
who grows bigger
each night
with the new child
getting ready
to come
into our
lives.

And I fear
with two babes
in the house
I'll have no
time at all
for me.

How will I
sleep the sleep
I need to be alert
in my office every morning,
or be free to walk the
solitary paths
I love?

Or find the time
to think my thoughts
with two like you
crying in the night
asking for
water
bears
and who knows
what else?

What
will I do then?

What will
I do?

Just breathe
in and out
and watch
my breath
go out and in
they say.

The teacher
Thich Nhat Hanh
tells
the tale
of another father
chasing down time
enough to satisfy
a rowdy son
newborn-daughter
wife
and self.

That father
meditates on breath
and finds some way to make
the time his children take
his own time too.

He gently twists
and bends the hard
dividing line
between "my afternoon"
"your morning"
between "work time,"
"play time" between "your time"
or "my time"
for all the things to do.

He relaxes
the boundaries
between "me"
and "you."

That father
stakes a claim
to the days and hours
he spends on baby baths
and bottles
games and tears and grins
even midnight
diaper changes—
as his time too.

So he finds
he now has
endless time.

Will I be able
to do that as well?

Only time
and breath
will tell.

"A wild patience has taken me this far."

ADRIENNE RICH

Bibliography

Asano, Kiichi, photographer, Takakuwa, Gisei, writer. *Invitation to Japanese Gardens*. Tokyo: Charles E. Tuttle, 1970

Bolen Shinoda, Jean. *The Tao of Psychology*. New York: Harper and Row, 1982.

Bolinger, Judith and English, Jane. *Waterchild*. London: Wildwood House, 1981.

Danielou, Alain. *Yoga*. New York: University Books, 1955.

Gerber, Magda, editor. *A Manual for Parents and Professionals*. Los Angeles: Resources for Infant Educarers, 1987.

Ginsberg, Allen. *Collected Poems 1947-1980*. New York: Harper & Row, 1984

Herrigel, Eugen. *Zen in the Art of Archery*. New York: Random House, 1989.

Kaplan, Justin. *Walt Whitman: A Life*. New York: Simon & Shuster, 1982.

Krishnamurti, J. *The First and Last Freedom*. Wheaton, Illinois: The Theosophical Publishing House, 1971.

Leggett, Trevor. *A First Zen Reader*. Rutland, Vermont: Charles E. Tuttle, 1987.

Lao Tsu, translation from the Chinese by Gia-Fu Feng and Jane English. *Tao Te Ching*. New York: Random House, 1972.

Mittwer, Henry. *The Art of Chabana*. Rutland, Vermont: Charles E. Tuttle, 1974.

Miura, Isshu and Fuller Sasaki, Ruth. *The Zen Koan*. San Diego: Harcourt Brace Jovanovich, 1965.

Nakamura, Julia V. *The Japanese Tea Ceremony*. Mount Vernon, New York: Peter Pauper Press, 1965.

Nhat Hanh, Thich. *The Miracle of Mindfulness*. Boston: Beacon Press, 1987.

Pirsig, Robert M. *Zen and the Art of Motorcycle Maintenance*. New York: Bantam, 1984.

Rich, Adrienne. *A Wild Patience Has Taken Me This Far*. New York: W.W. Norton, 1981.

Sangharakshita, Maha Sthavira. *The Essence of Zen*. Glasgow: Windhorse, 1985.

Sivaraksa, Sulak. *Seeds of Peace*. Berkeley: Parallax Press, 1992.

Stryk, Lucien and Ikemoto, Takashi, editor and translator. *The Penguin Book of Zen Poetry*. London: Penguin Books, 1981.

Suzuki, Daisetz Teitaro, D. Litt. *An Introduction to Zen Buddhism*. New York: Grove Press, 1934.

Suzuki, Shunryu. *Zen Mind, Beginner's Mind*. New York: Weatherhill, 1991.

Swami Vishnudevananda. *The Complete Illustrated Book of Yoga*. New York: Bell, 1959.

Swami Venkatesananda. *Yoga*. Auf Dem Heidchen, Germany: Sivananda Press, 1974.

Thompson, Paula. *Karma*. Los Angeles: Paula Thompson, 1991.

Van Gogh, Vincent. *Van Gogh, a Self-Portrait*, Letters revealing his life as a painter, selected by W.H. Auden. Greenwich, Connecticut: New York Graphic Society, 1961

Watts, Alan W. *The Spirit of Zen*. New York: Grove Press, 1960.

Whitman, Walt. *Leaves of Grass*. New York: The Modern Library, 1921.

Winokur, Jon, editor and compiler. *Zen to Go*. New York: Penguin Books, 1990.

Zukav, Gary. *The Dancing Wu Li Masters*. New York: Bantam Books, 1986.

Sarah Arsone is a journalist and poet living in Pacific Palisades, California. Her work has appeared in many newpapers and magazines including the *New York Times*, *Los Angeles Times Magazine*, *Working Mother Magazine*, *The London Sunday Times*, and the *Columbia Journalism Review*. She is active in the Los Angeles poetry scene.

Zen and the Art of Changing Diapers
was set in Goudy Oldstyle by Jim Cook
using Quark Xpress.

To order this book by phone, please call 1 (800) 275-2606.

To order by mail, please send $8.95 for each book and add $2.00 for the first book and $.50 for each additional book for postage and handling. Send check or money order to Sarah Arsone, ZEN AND THE ART OF CHANGING DIAPERS, P.O. Box 1486, Pacific Palisades, Ca, 90272.